SILENT FAITH

Finding

Assurance

In

The

Hidden

WADE A. WOOLFOLK

SILENT FAITH
Finding Assurance In The Hidden

Copyright © 2022 by Wade A. Woolfolk

Published by Wade A. Woolfolk

Woolfolk Enterprises LLC

WOOLFOLK
ENTERPRISES

ISBN: 979-8-9859782-3-0

Printed in the United States of America.

Dedication

To those whose faith is under attack.

<u>Scripture References</u>: All references to scripture in this book may be from the New International Version, King James Version, or New American Standard Bible.

<u>Photo Credit</u>: All photos depicted in this book are courtesy of www.tamiejohnson.com │ The Brand Studio.

Table of Contents

Introduction

Suddenly, I found myself running - dodging all kinds of obstacles and things in my path. I had to be aware of my surroundings. I looked in front of me, beside me, and behind me. Even when I heard things, I had to look above me, too. This was one of the scariest times of my life because I was running from an enemy unbeknownst to me. I was under attack. Then, I realized it was not me the enemy wanted after all. Instead, it was my faith.

The enemy wanted my faith because of its power. It wanted my faith because it is a representation, through me, of the highest power whom they know they cannot defeat. As a result of their insecurities, my faith was a threat to their very existence. The enemy knows it is my biggest weapon. Therefore, to regain their security, to continue to do the evil things that made them whole, it needed to come after me! The enemy needed to silence my faith.

Is this you? Have you ever felt like this? If you are reading this book, then I assume that you know your faith is under attack. There are some similarities between how I felt and the way you may feel, also. Now, more than ever, our faith is under attack by an enemy we can see and one whom we cannot.

The world has changed, but our God remains the same. No longer can we sit by and let our faith be vulnerable and deteriorate from the attempted attacks of the enemy.

I wrote this book to help guide you through some of the most common situations we face that the enemy may use to try and silence our faith. It is my prayer and hope that you will come out with a stronger and more enhanced level of faith to be prepared to fight!

Hebrews 11:1 says, *"Now faith is the substance of things hoped for; the evidence of things not seen."* I hope that by reading this book, your faith will become more substantive with the necessary depth you need to draw from in times of battling the enemy.

Together, we can find assurance in the hidden and keep our faith from being silenced.

Chapter 1: Recognize Your Power

How long did it take you to learn how to stand up for yourself? As a young child, were you ever teased or talked about? How did you handle it? When you go through life as a young child, there are so many things you have to deal with and learn. Especially when you are being teased or talked about, you have to learn how to recognize that it is happening, for one. Then, if you are not used to hearing negative things about yourself, you have to learn how to recognize that you are being disrespected.

Growing up, I had to deal with being bullied for a few of my elementary school years. It was particularly difficult because I did not know

"PEOPLE WILL TRY TO BOX YOU IN, IF YOU HELP THEM TO FOLD THE BOX."

how to recognize it. I was not used to hearing negative things being said about me. This was not a practice in my home with my parents. If anything, they tried to do everything in their power to encourage me and tell me positive things about how much they thought of me. In that regard, I consider myself to be very blessed.

1

I started in a private school. What was interesting was that I skipped kindergarten and went from pre-school straight into the first grade. Therefore, I was a year ahead of my friends, but that also meant that I was a year behind in maturity. Starting school at an earlier age, trust me – you do not know a thing about life and, especially, how to interact effectively with other kids older than you. I attended a private Baptist school from first to third grade.

It was a school steeped in traditional Baptist and Christian practices. We would say the Pledge of Allegiance every morning (when you could still say it, of course); but we also said a pledge to the Christian flag that adorned every classroom. I believe the hymns we sang each morning were *Holy, Holy, Holy*, and *Onward Christian Soldiers*. It was a school that provided me with a good foundation of Christian principles.

At the end of third grade, I remember telling my parents that I did not want to go back to that school. It was not anything that happened that led to this decision on my part. There was nothing related to my grades that said I was struggling or could not handle the coursework at this school. The main reason why I skipped kindergarten was that I could already read very well at a young age.

For me, the decision to change was because I no longer wanted to deal with the structure. Later, I would find out that part of the reason was also that one day my babysitter left me out in the rain after school. Yes, you read that correctly.

At the start of my fourth-grade year, I began it at a local public school. It was exciting to not have to worry about wearing a uniform every day anymore! I could wear my regular clothes and my favorite sneakers, although my parents never really focused on brand-name stuff for me. It was peaceful knowing that I could make new friends; some of which lived in my same neighborhood. Well, little did I know that things would drastically change.

Bullying, according to www.stopbullying.gov, is defined as "...*unwanted, aggressive behavior among school-aged children that involves a real or perceived power imbalance. The behavior is repeated, or has the potential to be repeated, over time.*"

Quite simply, bullying is about power.

So, here I am in my new school, trying to make new friends. However, something seems to be a little different from my days in private school. I noticed that kids were not looking at me the same. They were looking at me as if I were some sort of endangered species or from outer space. Questions start to get directed to me and they mostly centered around my hair. Those who know me know that my grade of hair is a direct representation of my mixed heritage.

I would get questions from girls, such as "Can I touch your hair?" Not realizing why, and wanting to impress them, I answered "sure! Of course!" After a while, I realized that kids at this school were just not used to seeing a boy like me with my grade of hair.

It became even more puzzling when some of the other boys, that were not used to seeing it either, began to make fun of me every day. Many thought I was from a foreign country. I would often get questions, such as "Hey, where's your green card?" A Green Card, of course, is a document confirming a person's identity, from another country, showing that this person has permanent residency in the United States. Being born in Washington, DC, and raised in Maryland, of course, I knew I was not from a foreign country.

However, the jokes continued with comparisons to characters of Native American descent, such as Geronimo who was a prominent leader and medicine man from the Bedonkohe band of the Apache people. It extended to the fictional character of Tonto from the Lone Ranger western television series and movies. Although, the one that perplexed me was the comparison to Mahatma Gandhi.

I did not know much about Gandhi at this time, of course; however, after learning about him later in life, I saw that he was all about nonviolence. He was instrumental in trying to secure India's independence from British rule and he was someone that was admired by the Rev. Dr. Martin Luther King, Jr.

So, in that regard, the comparison is cool. The thing that puzzled me, however, was that everyone teased me about my hair and compared me to Gandhi, but Gandhi did not have any hair at all! I thought, "How can I be compared to him?!" I just did not understand why these jokes continued to happen to me.

It was so bad that eventually I went to my parents and asked them if I was adopted. They could not believe that I was asking this question. Well, it went so deep that doubt began to enter my mind about who I was and where I came from. My parents are both from Virginia, and my mother is brown-skinned and my father is lighter fair-skinned but you can tell both are African-American.

As the fourth grade continued, there came a time when the same boys that joked about my hair and heritage began to bully me even more. I guess because I did not do much to stop them from talking about me, perhaps they felt they had some sort of power over me.

Every day my mom packed a lunch for me in my lunchbox. I was a big Star Wars fan (still am today) so I had an *Empire Strikes Back* lunchbox that would eventually get destroyed in a school kickball game.

I know…don't ask!

We would put our lunchboxes in our assigned cubbyholes at school. Usually, I would have a sandwich with some sort of dessert included. At first, the individual would ask me if they could have my dessert. Being nice and trying to fit in, too, I guess I did not put up much of a fuss.

Then, it started to happen a few times a week to the point where he would not even ask me anymore. He was not from the same neighborhood and was much bigger than me. I was such a small, skinny kid at the time. I guess, when I look back on it, I was probably afraid to confront him, fearing that he might retaliate by fighting.

I finally let my parents know this was happening, and if you are a parent that has been through a situation where your child has been bullied, then you know they were not very happy. I believe there was a phone conversation among the parents, along with myself and the boy involved to make sure that he would not take my lunch anymore and the situation got better. Just when I thought things would take a turn for the better, I ended up having an altercation with a sixth grader.

So, one day I step out of class to go use the bathroom. As I am going in, a much taller sixth grader, whose name I never knew, thought I approached him confrontationally. In other words, he thought I flinched or bucked my shoulders at him. He proceeded to get mad and starts punching me right in the doorway inside the bathroom. I cannot do anything but drop to the floor and try to protect myself as he began to kick me, too.

The only thing that saved me was someone else coming into the bathroom. Luckily, it was someone I knew and he helped me up and took me back to class. At this point, not only is it me and my classmate walking back to the class but I was also accompanied by a fresh black eye! As soon as I hit the classroom door, I began to cry and the teacher took me to the principal's office.

I remember that we had a parent-student conference with the guy and his family. The only thing I remembered is that his parents grounded him for the whole summer. I thought, wow...that was a serious punishment! I could not imagine being punished for an entire summer.

When I think about bullying, somehow it reminds me of the story of David and Goliath.

As you may know, the story is centered around two tribes: the Israelites and the Philistines. They could not get along and planned to battle each other.

The Philistines, it is estimated, had a 9-foot-tall threat named Goliath. He was cocky and confident and demanded a battle from the Israelites for about forty days. Goliath was just itching to start some trouble. David, who was a small shepherd boy, decided that he would step up for the Israelites and fight the giant. Goliath heard this news and laughed. He mocked David for being small in stature. However, what Goliath did not know was that David had God on his side.

Walking to battle, David stopped by a stream and picked up five small stones for his slingshot. As the battle began, David took one of the stones and fired it at Goliath, hitting him in his head and killing the 9-foot giant. What is it that we need to know about this story and how it relates to bullying? Well, let me provide you with a few takeaways to tie it all together.

People will try to box you in, especially if you help them to fold the box.
My first thought is we should not let anyone try to place us in a category or a position for which we are not comfortable. When I did not do anything to stop my

classmate from taking my lunch, I am sure he placed me in the category of being afraid or even weak. He probably saw me as someone who could be taken advantage of regularly.

When King Saul was getting David prepared for battle, he dressed him in his tunic and put armor and a large helmet on his head. David found the items to be too bulky and too much. He was not used to wearing them and did not want to wear them. Therefore, he took them off.

We have to be careful not to let people try to put labels on us or make us do things that we are not used to doing or things that we are not called to do. When I was being bullied, people were trying to take advantage of me or label me as something with a derogatory connotation – simply because I let them and did not know any better.

Wisdom can also be our weapon.
The second thought is that, occasionally, we have to exercise wisdom over our physical battles. David knew that the armor King Saul was trying to give him was not going to work for him. Using his clothes, the only thing David needed was his shepherd stick and five stones for his slingshot. He utilized wisdom to his advantage.

A lot of times, when going into battle we do not adhere to what God says we need. We go into our battles thinking we need more than we do. By following our lead, we can cause unnecessary confusion when it is not from God. Having discernment and understanding of God's voice, we can exercise wisdom unlike any other in our battles and it can also be our weapon to defeat the enemy.

We need a slingshot kind of faith.

As followers of Jesus Christ, it is essential to have faith and courage to stand up to anything or anyone. What are you taking with you into battle?

The world, if we let it, will try to silence our faith. Sometimes we just have to pull back; take a step back, evaluate through God's eyes and His Word, and use the stones (the Scriptures) God has given us to fight. Battling a 9-foot giant, anyone would think we need something big to fight. Not David. With God on his side, all he needed was a few stones and his faith to defeat Goliath.

We often have what we believe to be '9-foot problems' in our lives. Even though, in reality, they may only be 4-foot problems. So, what makes our problems seem bigger than they are? It is simple – our clouded faith can make our problems seem larger than they are. When we do not rely on our faith to fight or hand over all of our problems to God, everything can seem larger than it may be.

Bullying has become a serious problem in our world.

It can lead to long-lasting physical and emotional problems. Serious problems, such as anxiety, depression, and other health concerns can surface. With the increase in cyberbullying, our kids are at risk more than ever.

The pitfalls of social media can be detrimental for our kids' young minds (underdeveloped minds) to try and handle. Although bullying may not necessarily be linked to suicide, if we are not careful chronic bullying can lead to poor choices and decisions that can affect the lives of our children.

We must continue to recognize our power and believe in ourselves and fight the good fight. Knowing that we are in a good fight with the Deliverer of the Good News, there is nothing we cannot accomplish with God.

Chapter 2: Redeem Your Past

D o you ever run into someone whom you previously dated where the courtship did not go so well? Have you ever seen a former friend across a crowded room at a function and decided to go in another direction, because you did not want to deal with them? I am pretty certain that, like myself, you may have been in situations similar to this at least one time in your life.

This, unfortunately, is how we can deal with things from our past. It is like that former girlfriend

"WE CAN LET OUR PAST TURN INTO A HOSTAGE SITUATION."

or boyfriend that, if we saw them on the street and it was not a good experience or memory, we would want to walk right past them or in another direction.

What is it about our past and how we deal with people and situations that can haunt us?

I believe one of the reasons why we experience so much difficulty is that we, sometimes unknowingly, continue to breathe life into our past. Our past is supposed to be the past – a distant memory. Things we have been through, chapters we thought we have closed; some of us can actually resuscitate these things. In the extreme, some of us want the past back so much that we can operate like a defibrillator to pump life back into it.

I have never been a big fan of taking backwards steps. I believe that, if you have followed ordered steps, then that is the way you should go. Even if those steps were not ordered, you should not have any regrets about the path, the journey that has led you to this point; however, some of us cannot see past this way of thinking and we often do things that are not ordered, which can cause us more distress than the first time.

In my book *Yea, Though I Walk: Experiencing God in Every Step of Life*, one of the chapters touches on being stuck on what used to be. It talks about the story of Lot and Sodom and Gomorrah.

I believe this can be so true in this regard. We become so fixated on the past and how it made us feel, we are willing to accept it again, no matter the negativity that came along with it. This was a lesson I learned early in life. Depending on how we feel about ourselves, our self-esteem, the desperation that we have can lead us to forget how we were treated during the experience and the feeling of emptiness we were left with to feel.

During the middle of my career, I was working for a thriving small consulting firm. Over time, I worked to be promoted from an associate to a manager. It was pretty fulfilling, although stressful at times. There was so much that I learned that I began to feel empowered.

After a while, I decided to leave this company for something more centric to the communications field, which was a growing passion of mine, at the time. Upon leaving, I was so excited that I shared what I was going to be doing, how valued I felt; I even shared my new office view with a few individuals, which had a window by a man-made lake. I began to believe that *I* did this and *I* had now made it!

After some time, to my disappointment I began to realize that the only reason the new company wanted me was because of the relationships I had with certain federal agencies. It had nothing to do with my talent, but everything to do with whom I knew in hopes of gaining new contracts. Needless to say, the new dream job was turning into a nightmare.

The powers that be began to pick on every little thing relating to what I wrote, my communication style, and ideas in general. It was like a case was being built for my departure. Being still young in my professional experience, I knew something was happening, but I did not know how to fight it.

Nevertheless, the day finally came where I was called into the board room for a conversation. After they pointed out my "inconsistencies" that they had purposely been building, they said that this relationship was not working out. I responded that I agreed and that the six-figure salary I was receiving was not worth the headaches and the disturbance of my peace. Instead of firing me, they gave me the option to resign.

Now, you might think "wow, that is a gracious company." On the contrary, what I did not tell you was that in my interviews with the company, they touted that they had never fired anyone. That's right. You read that correctly. Of course, you hear that as a young professional and think that is an awesome statistic. It might raise a red flag to most, but more than likely you may overlook it because it sounded like there was security in your job. Needless to say, it more or less represented a false sense of security.

When companies fire people, that goes on record with various labor entities that keep track of this kind of information. By mutually agreeing to dissolve the working relationship or getting people to resign, it helped to keep this company's name pretty clean as a "good place to work," which helps with the company's public image and value to its stockholders.

After looking back on the whole situation, I realize that is exactly what they were doing. There is not a company in existence or one that no longer exists, for that matter, that can truly say that they have never fired anyone.

So, here I am with no job and a two-month severance package. Do I eat crow and go back to the place I left? Needless to say, I had to swallow my pride and realize that I had made a mistake. I made a decision that was not ordained by God. I did not pray on it, nor did I seek God's word when making the decision to join this firm. It was made out of emotion and the thought of feeling valued to obtain a six-figure salary. Therefore, this part of my past haunted me because I was left wondering what might have been had I stayed with the firm that I left. How far could I have gone in my career?

Nevertheless, as I spiritually mature, I realize that I cannot have regrets about the path I have traveled and neither can you. In Isaiah 43:18-19, it says *"Forget the former things; do not dwell on the past. See, I am doing a new thing!"*

The 43rd chapter of Isaiah is interesting because it focuses on how we view our past. God is calling Israel to the carpet about the miracles that have occurred. The blind that can see, the deaf who can hear; who else could do this but God, is the thinking here. In their ways, Israel turned away from God and put their belief in other gods. God wants Israel to prove their case or accept that He is the one who has delivered, just as He did when He parted the Red Sea. As a result of God's forgiving nature, He decided to bring down those considered fugitives and judge Babylon accordingly, fully redeeming the people of Israel.

That is the God we serve. Even when we do not deserve to be redeemed because of our selfishness, He can extend that mercy to us.

Despite my unemployment, I decided to start my own company and step out there on faith. It was a struggle, but I learned a lot of things and I learned a lot about myself. After about two years, I decided that I needed to get back into the workforce, because the money I was earning through my company was not coming as fast as I would have liked.

Due to my faith in stepping out on my own, God blessed me with a chance meeting over lunch, that was about business, but eventually turned into an employment opportunity. God redeemed my self-esteem and let me know that my decision to work for the company that did not work out was all in the past. My feet were back on solid ground and I had no reason to silence my faith.

Let me share with you what I took away from this whole experience.

We can let our past turn into a hostage situation.

I know you have seen those movies where, time and time again, the criminals will do what they do. Then, for some reason everything turns in a different direction and they end up taking a hostage, often becoming cornered with nowhere to go. Dealing with our past can have this same effect on us and can truly silence our faith. If our relationship with God is not where it should be, we can panic. We can start to think about doing desperate things.

We put demands on people that we feel have caused us to be in this situation or have caused us some pain. Not to mention, sometimes innocent people who mean a lot to us can get caught up in the crossfire of our anger and desperation.

The good thing is that our God is a forgiving God. We do not have to negotiate our way out of these situations. We do not have to make a list of demands because whatever we have done, God has already forgiven us. It is our lack of connection to God and our human nature that can turn us into hostages of our own past.

You are not the definition of your past.
When we think about our past, we can get caught up in a chronological account of self-persecution. If we are not careful, if we do not recognize this happening at the time, we can easily let our past define who we are and who we

become. It is almost as if we can take a dictionary and look up the word 'past' and see our personal life mistakes and mishaps defined right there on the page. We are not the poster child of the errors of our past. The biggest mistake we can make is to let the world define us.

When we let our past define us, we give it power over us. The authority of our life, which belongs to God, we transfer it to the life events that have accumulated over time. It is like signing a permission slip to go on a lifetime field trip to the "Museum of Self-persecution." And there we are…defined in the pages of life, defined in the portraits and statues of the halls of persecution as someone bitter or someone that always feels the world owes us something.

Where we come from, not just environmentally but also our upbringing, helps to shape the character and strength of who we are. It does not define or serve as the catalyst of who we are to become. Our belief and faith in God, along with the belief in ourselves is what sets our soul and purpose on the right track.

Our faith can ignite God's redemptive power.

Let me say that God does not truly need any help from us to do anything. What God desires is a trusting and faithful heart for Him. Our God is a God of mercy and grace. Our belief in Him automatically puts us in the pool of blessings. When we have turned away from God, it does not remove us from this pool; however, we move from the deep end of bountiful blessings to the shallow end. What I am really saying is that when we turn away from God, our blessings can be delayed. The good news is that this is not permanent, because of the nature of God.

God wants our faith. He does not want it to be silenced. He wants us in that hostage situation to turn to no one else but Him. How do we show our desire for Him? When we have done wrong, how do we show that God can continue to count on us? We do this through faith, which then ignites God's redemption for the sins that we have committed.

That pool of blessings will turn into an overflowing river of blessings so big that you will not be able to keep up! We will move away from the shallow end.

As you will read in the 43rd chapter of Isaiah, God promised that the people of Israel could pass through rivers and fire without being drowned or getting burned. That same redemptive love can be extended to us just by releasing ourselves from our past and showing our faith that God has forgiven us. If our faith is silenced, how will God be reassured of our desire for His love?

What we have to do is to first accept that our past is the past. It's over! No matter how much we contemplate everything that has occurred and played it out over and over in our minds, it is done. We think about all of the things we could do differently. We get stuck on the "what ifs" and "maybe I should've" thoughts.

The thing to remember is that we cannot change what has been done, but we can change what we do next! When we let go of our hostage situation and realize the past does not define us, we can begin to let God do that "new thing!" That same new thing he promised to the people of Israel can be ours, too. The promise of renewing His love for us; the promise of a redeeming grace.

Chapter 3: Evaluate Your Faith in Friends

W hat does it mean to be a friend in this day and age? There is so much to learn about friendship as we move through life. As we evolve, the meaning of friendship does the same, moving through levels and tiers. Just as we move through schooling in life, friendship can have elementary (or beginning stages) to middle of the road or testing the waters of adulthood, similar to how we experience middle school and high school.

However, as an adult, friendship takes on a new meaning to which something is always to be learned. It is almost like a college of friendship.

When you are a child, making what you believe to be a friend is pretty easy. It does not take much

"GOOD FRIENDS WILL GO THROUGH THE FIRE WITH YOU."

conversation to get a friendship started. It can be as simple as playing in the sandbox, playing football, riding someone's bike, or asking to play with one of their toys. Then, there is the imaginative interaction that almost seems natural or instinctive like pretending you are fighting in some kind of space war with ships or some military combat mission with the latest action figures. At least for boys, this was my experience. For girls, it may be something relating to hopscotch, jumping rope, or playing with dolls. It is so easy to make friends when you are a child.

As you get just a little older, it takes more conversation. Likes and dislikes become more discoverable. A little more fighting can come into play. It is still easy to get along, but it can change a little quicker than before. I should know. I think I fought two people I grew up with in my neighborhood! The good thing is that we are friends today.

When you get to middle school and high school age, that is when the friendships (existing and new) become more meaningful. I guess it is because you can get introduced to different aspects of what adults may experience. Personalities are more formed and developed. Crushes materialize to what we think is love. You witness more about relationships through your family. Opinions about different things mean a lot more as you matriculate through these ages.

College is a whole different experience, as you are looked at as a young adult. With this young adult title, you are a little more set in your ways and your personality and character are almost shaped to how you are going to be as an adult. Friendships are more mature in certain ways, but then you also have your friends that you like to cut up with every now and then.

Once you get into your adult years, that is when friendships can vary a lot. There are some people that may evolve and some that may not. Some of your friendships may grow and become more meaningful and some may not. They may become stagnant or they can dissipate altogether. Political views, religious beliefs and philosophies, platonic relationships between men and women; education levels; economic status; all of these things can influence some friendships depending on their strength.

Yes, friendship is an ever-changing learning experience. It is something I doubt that any of us may ever master completely. One thing is for sure, the word gives us plenty of examples to think about when it comes to friendships and how they can try to silence our faith.

The weight of friendships can be heavy for those not in shape to lift.

Ecclesiastes 4:10 says, *"If either of them falls down, one can help the other up. But pity anyone who falls and has no one to help them up."* There is no secret that in life we all will experience some hardship at some point. In some cases, the hardship may be tougher than others will ever experience.

In the darkest of times, your friends are representatives of God's Kingdom that can be there for you. Some friends, their spiritual gift may be providing words of encouragement to help get you through the rough spots. It may be a phone call, a text, a quick email just to check on you. Some may lend you money if you ask and those kinds of friends are godsends! Those with an accountable spirit may want to do something different, such as wanting to get you out of the house or grab a quick bite to eat over some meaningful and helpful conversation. Some may even want to pray with you on a daily basis or at least once a week.

Additionally, there are people whom you may consider a friend, but they may not consider you to be a friend at the same level in which you hold the value of friendship. In other words, you can think of yourself as a highly-valued friend to someone; however, that friend may not hold his/her friendship with you having that same value.

Let's be honest – sometimes we do certain things for friends in which they value the friendship because you are doing these things. When you are going through something, these friends may be wishing you the best in recovery, constantly checking on you, or even going the extra mile to visit or ensure that you have everything you need. Definitely not a bad thing for a friend to do, right? However, you may have some that are only doing these things so that you can get well to continue doing those things for them. For some, expending yourself to be a friend is not a heavy lift, when it comes to getting or expecting something in return.

For some, helping you through the rough spots can be a heavy lift depending on where they are in the friendship and in their relationship with God. This is not a bad thing. It is just a fact that different friends can provide different feelings. As a believer and a friend, we must accept where our friends are and continue to love and accept them for who they are.

When you are down and out, a friend can lift you up.

Dealing with the loss of a loved one is something hard for anyone to handle. However, if you have a good friend by your side, it is something that can help to see you through. When we lose someone close to us, many things go through our minds, we experience many emotions.

Especially with the difficulties that families have to experience during this time, it can cause family members to react differently and sometimes negatively, in certain instances. Having a good friend to talk to occasionally can help you better cope with the situation.

Job 16:20-21 says, *"My intercessor is my friend as my eyes pour out tears to God; on behalf of a man, he pleads*

with God as one pleads for a friend." This scripture talks
about having a friend to be an intercessor or an arbitrator
while you are trying to heal from your loss.

One story in The Bible (2 Samuel 10:2) shows the
comforting friendship of David. He had a friend named
Hanun who lost his father, Nahash. David was fond of
Nahash because of how he treated him. Therefore, in the
time of grief that Hanun was experiencing, David sent
ambassadors to express condolences and sympathy to
Hanun and his family. This act of kindness, or some may
even say an act of ministerial importance, demonstrates
how a friend can support in times of grief. It is important to
remember that your relationship with people can extend
grace and blessings to others. This is why we should
always treat people in a way that we wish to be treated.

In my book, *Yea, Though I Walk*, I spoke about how I
encountered a stranger that had a heart attack and passed
away right in front of me. After calling 9-1-1 and having
them walk me through CPR procedures, I prayed over the
individual's soul with The Lord's Prayer. A few days later,
I met with the family of the individual and also prayed with
them because I was the last person to pray over their
father's soul. God will send you to be a friend among
strangers in the time of need. God sent me in that moment
to be a friend.

Good friends will go through the fire with you.

When times get tough, it is good to know that you can have friends that will support you throughout the tough times. In the toughest of times, you can learn who is on your side and who may not be as supportive as you thought. Again, this is not anything to be upset about or a cause to end a friendship. It just simply illustrates where people may be in their lives.

Everyone has heard of the story of Shadrach, Meshach, and Abednego in the book of Daniel. In case you have not, these three men were Hebrew men that were thrown into a fiery furnace by the King of Babylon, Nebuchadnezzar II, all because they would not bow down to the image of the king. At the utter amazement of the king, the three men did not burn or die. In fact, there was a fourth figure that appeared in the fire, which is believed to be the Son of God. At the recommendation of Daniel, Nebuchadnezzar brought the young men out of the furnace and promoted them to be in charge of all affairs in the province of Babylon.

When things are tough, we can count on our faith to see us through, even in the most sweltering times of our lives, but it is also good to have a friend to vouch for you like Daniel did for the three men. If we have someone on our side, who truly has our best interest at heart in the spirit of

God, we can feel supported in those difficult times. Together, our faith can bring us out of those times and God can elevate us to higher levels.

The previous items are just some examples of how friends can support us and not allow our faith to be silenced when things get tough. However, it would not be right if we did not show the other side and focus on difficulties we can have with friends.

One of the hardest things to do in life is to fit in with the crowd. Social scenes may not be a person's strong suit, but it is something that we all have to navigate in our lives. This includes attending different things and supporting other friends in their endeavors. However, what we can often experience is neglect and overlook.

For example, maybe we did not get invited to a particular wedding or graduation event. Perhaps it was a family or friend cookout invite that somehow did not make it to our email or text messages. The confused feelings we have may be the result of our drummed up false sense of security about where our level of friendship or love in the family actually stood. For whatever reason, when we do not get included, it can hit us like a ton of bricks, depending on our spiritual maturity and where we are in the relationships.

If we cannot immediately point to a reason, we will start to rewind life in our minds and try to figure out what we did to someone that might have caused us to be overlooked. Don't do this. When we start to do this, it can cause us extra stress and worry, and even anger in some instances which is never healthy.

What we need to do is to learn to be okay if we do not get included or considered. We must adapt to the mindset that we will be okay if we are not in the count or do not make the cut. Is something so important that it is worth sacrificing your physical health and peace of mind? The same may go for your career. If you did not get considered for a particular project or position, do not worry. It's okay! Exercise your faith in that maybe not getting selected was a blessing in disguise and God has something better in store for you.

Additionally, a lot of times we put too much expectation on our friends and when they fall short or cannot meet our criteria for being deemed a "friend," we end up with an attitude about them and just cut them off.

It is ideal to have friends that we can count on whenever we have problems; however, I believe we make the mistake of relying too much on that friend trying to solve our problems. Or, we even look to them to tell us what we want to hear; and when they do not, we are quick to write them off as friends.

All along, I believe that our approach should be to find a friend to be a supportive arm to our problems, but not the solver. That expectation is something we should transfer to God, to be the way maker in our lives. We need to focus on finding those friends that will be with us while we go through our problems, go through the fire, and help us to not face them alone.

Another dynamic that has transformed what friendship means is social media. It is amazing how since 2007, when social media started becoming popular, the cultural norms and myths that have been birthed. So many people are caught up in how many friend requests or "friends" they have acquired; how many likes or comments they receive on their posts and videos. It is amazing how much effort is put into developing a social media persona.

Personally, I have tried to create a social media persona and following; however, I cannot see sitting at the computer or on my phone all day trying to get people's attention to like me or make money. Maybe that is just me and my old school way of thinking! I leave that hustle to the younger crowd, as they can do it in their sleep.

However, if anyone sincerely journeys with me via social media, I hope it is because of the friend I am or the words I use that may inspire you, and I am certainly happy to have you walking with me in this journey of life.

But what is a friend in the social media world? It is a legitimate question that affects our society in every way. 1 Thessalonians 5:11 says, *"Therefore encourage one another and build one another up, just as you are doing."*

Social media has done some great things to bring people and groups of people together. However, it has also led to the creation and dissolution of friendships and families. It has led to kinships and disagreements on various topics that have destroyed our traditional definition of friends.

The constant stream of information – posts, instant messages, stories, reels, links shared; the list goes on and on. The immediacy of information - it is a lot for our minds to process and still maintain friendships and relationships. It is something we were not used to in the beginning; however, some of us have it down to a science or can manage everything at reasonable levels. In my opinion, I believe it has taken the personal touch of friendships out of the equation. Nevertheless, as more social media platforms are developed, it will add to the complexity of how we view friendships.

Friends, acquaintances, influencers, and business partners may be titles that people in our networks hold. Whatever it may be and as you re-evaluate your faith in friends, we should always look to encourage one another and not tear down anyone. You never know what people are going through or what cross they have to carry.

Chapter 4: Commit to Your Faith

One of the worst things you can do as an individual is to be content with who you are and have a silenced faith that does not allow you to see who you can become.

It is human nature to struggle with our self-esteem. Whether you had a decent childhood or maybe it was not the best childhood, at some point you can find yourself questioning if who you are today is who you are supposed to be.

As a part of this struggle, many people feel like "well…I am the way that I am." Almost as if

"LOVING WHO YOU ARE MEANS ACCEPTING WHERE YOU HAVE BEEN."

they are settling for the way they are and feeling like there is nothing they can do about it now.

Why do we do this to ourselves?

Why do we torture or give up on ourselves?

Why are we so afraid to be great?

One suggestion for this is that some people may have what is called *apprehensive behavior.*

According to Dictionary.com, *apprehensive behavior* can be defined as *threat assessing and imagining something bad or unpleasant might happen.*

Now, let me say that I am not a psychologist, but, in my opinion, apprehensive reactions are not meant to be a bad thing. It is normal to react apprehensively when we encounter things that might do us harm.

For example, if we have a bill coming due soon, but our bank account does not have enough to cover it, our apprehensive behavior will kick in. We may move some money over from our savings account. We may try to work extra hours at a part-time job to help make ends meet. Depending on the size of the bill, we may have to obtain a small loan to cover everything. Our apprehensive behavior kicks us into survival mode.

Or, you may notice that you have been having headaches lately – more often than usual. This could be something of concern that makes you apprehensive. You might decide to exercise more because you think it just may be a lot of stress. You may contact your doctor to schedule an appointment to see what's going on.

Another apprehensive behavior could be a wife that has not heard from her husband in a while and it is getting late in the day. She would have reason to be apprehensive and worry and perhaps call him to make sure he is okay.

As I have stated, having apprehensive behavior is not meant to be a bad thing; however, what makes it bad is the continuous practice of it to the point where it begins to create levels of anxiety. Dictionary.com defines anxiety (in the psychiatry sense) as *a state of apprehension and psychic tension occurring in some forms of mental disorder*. With the growing state of anxiety, in the human sense eventually fear will follow.

One of the most remembered scriptures in The Bible is 2 Timothy 1:7, which says, *"For the Spirit God gave us does not make us timid, but gives us power, love and self-discipline."* We look at this verse and we say...okay, we should not be fearful about anything. Whatever comes at us in life, we should not be afraid. And these are good thoughts to have about this text, as it exhibits some level of faith. However, if you read the entire chapter, you will see that it takes on a different connotation.

What surrounds this text is the fact that the Apostle Paul is pouring into Timothy confidence to never give up about sharing his testimony of God nor about Paul being God's prisoner. Paul was pleading to Timothy to not let the flame, meaning his desire and will to preach about the gospel of Christ, die out. He did not want his faith to be silenced. He knew this was something that was entrusted in Timothy from his upbringing and influence of his family.

Paul's letter was essentially saying that if you have lost something, it is never too late to turn it around and begin again. You can start new today.

This is what I want you to understand, as well. Do not let fear silence your faith and keep you from being what God wants you to be. You have to commit to your faith. Here are some helpful thoughts to keep us from being fearful about starting over.

It is better to walk in dry sand than to stand in wet cement.

So many times, we focus on how things are right now. The way things are currently happening and how the current outlook may present itself. The time we take focusing on what is happening allows us to slow our progress to the point where we feel like we cannot start over. The longer we take, the more we can eventually become stuck.

It is that element of anxiety that leads to fear that slows us down to the point we stop moving forward altogether, which is similar to trying to walk in wet cement. Ultimately, we do not realize that the cement will sooner or later dry and become hardened to the point that we cannot move at all and could really damage ourselves. However, if we look at things from the perspective of walking in dry sand, we can continue to move no matter what is taking place. Sure, the hindrance of the sand may still make it difficult to walk at times, but at least you are able to keep moving forward.

We do not have to let people silence our faith where we no longer move forward with God or for God. Having presumptuous thoughts that we are stuck with how things appear now does not have to happen. What we need to understand is that life is everchanging and we can change with it at any time.

Are you celebrated or tolerated?

Often times, life can happen to us because of the situations that arise; some situations where we may be the cause of them. Think about yourself growing up in your parents' house or someone you know that grew up in their parents' house. There were probably some times where parents and children did not get along in certain instances. For example, children wanting to go out with friends whom parents may not approve; staying out late with friends in order to be considered cool; or dating someone whom your parents were not very fond of. The list goes on and on.

Well, all of these things may add up over time or fester into something much bigger. It may cause children to move

out of the home and try to experience life on their own –
sometimes before they are ready.

This is what happened in the parable of the prodigal
son, in Luke 15:20-24.

A son asked his father for his inheritance and lived
recklessly with it; squandering everything. He ran out of
money and had to work as a pig farmer. In fact, he got so
impoverished that he began to eat what the pigs ate. Can
you imagine that? I guess his apprehensive behavior began
to kick in, right!

Well, not long after that, he began to realize that his
father's servants lived and worked in better conditions than
where he worked. I imagine he took a look at where he was
and realized it was not all that. Therefore, he humbled
himself, went back to his father, and asked him for
forgiveness. With so much elation, his father welcomed
him with open arms and forgave him to his son's surprise.

The prodigal son realized that in his current situation,
he was not being celebrated. He was tolerating everything
that was happening around him, but it was not like what he
had at home with his father.

The prodigal son did not feel like he was stuck just
because his current situation was not good. He kept
walking in the dry sand to move forward, and eventually
got up enough nerve and faith to go back to his father. He

wanted to start over and did not let his current situation stifle him or silence his faith.

Sometimes we have to go where we are celebrated and not tolerated. There are situations we end up in where other individuals cannot see the real value of who we are. In life, we can run into people that are just focused on what they see on the surface. However, our value lies in our hearts and souls, and the things we say and do that make up our spirituality. When our value is reduced, or we perceive it to be reduced, we can get stuck with what currently is and become afraid to start again.

One of the things that people notice about me is that I like to wear suits. It is something that started when I was in college. As a person majoring in business, at times I felt compelled to go to class wearing a suit or at least a shirt and tie. Yes, there were a number of days where I stood out like a sore thumb! But it helped me to focus and begin to get into a business mindset. This is something that I carried to every job I have had in my career. A couple of times, I even had a part-time job where I have sold men's suits.

Although, a drawback is that sometimes this is all that people on the job have seen or felt about me. I would often hear, "You are really sharp!" or "Wade always dresses really nice."

I remember one job where I was the only African-American male in the department. Whenever something relating to the black culture came up, one supervisor would always ask my opinion. It would have been nice if it was all related to work. But sometimes it would be related to things like hip-hop clothes or rap music – things that had nothing to do with the professional environment.

I am thankful that God has provided and allowed me to have a decent professional wardrobe and perspective on my culture, but sometimes it felt like my substance was getting overlooked, which made things really frustrating for me. It could really make my blood boil sometimes.

One time, I was a project manager and was on a call with two senior individuals. I suggested that they should provide some communication because of their position and status and the probability that it would be better received than coming from me. One of the senior people disagreed and said to me, "No. This is why we have you. You are our whipping boy." In other words, they wanted me to take the brunt of the questions that would come. I was shocked. I had to look up the term. It was the most humiliating and blatant term I had ever heard in a professional environment.

No matter how smart I was or how much thought and perspective I would bring to projects, it did not matter.

Sometimes you can be celebrated for the wrong reasons and it is up to you if you wish to tolerate it.

Loving who you are, means accepting where you have been.

Do you love who you have become? Do you have regrets about the path you have taken in life? Loving who you are means that you have an inner peace about your moral character and values; your achievements; how you treat family; how you help people along the way.

All of these things are shaped by your experiences. They are molded by the paths that you have traveled in your life.

The truth is, a lot of people wish that they could do things much differently if they had the chance. I have heard many people say "What if I chose to go to another school?" "I wonder how different my life would be had I chosen the other job offer, instead of this one?"

What ends up happening is that people begin to build a regrettable attitude. If a life filled with regrets begins to fester and consumes your personality, it can then turn into bitterness and, possibly, even jealousy.

Not accepting who you have become, nor understanding the experiences that make up who you are, is like saying that God wasted His time in giving you the life you have. It is like saying God died on the cross for us for no reason.

The more you accept the paths that you have traveled and focus on the mistakes and growth lessons, the more you can begin to love yourself. Loving God and others all starts with how you view and love yourself.

In this chapter, we have focused on one of the most important elements of not having a silent faith – starting over. If you think about it, when you want to start over, you are already feeling like you are defeated…like the devil has taken you down and you cannot fight anymore.

However, once you start to change your mindset that you can get up from being knocked down, you are already giving your faith a voice. You are saying to the devil that there is nothing you can do to me that will make me stop believing that God can deliver!

One of the most interesting words one can learn to understand when it comes to starting over is the word '*circumstance*.' As we talked about, we tend to focus a lot on what is happening now. When we break down the word *circumstance*, we see that the word '*stance*' is a part of it. This means that there is a position. It is our position. And when things are tough, we can become fixated in this stance or this position.

But what we do not realize is that the first part of that
word is '*circum*,' which, means '*around*.' Therefore, when
we view the word circumstance, it is clear that a
circumstance is something that is not meant to be
permanent.

The same holds true for our situations that may look
impossible to overcome. Although they may look hard to
overcome in the flesh, with the Holy Spirit on our side
there is nothing that God cannot do to help us move beyond
our circumstances.

The main thing about starting over is that often times
we feel like we are starting from nothing. Wrong! Some of
us have a lifetime of examples and experiences that serve
as a spring board for starting over. You are not starting
from scratch. You are starting from a plethora of
experience and wisdom. Commit to your faith and you are
well on your way to starting a new path!

Chapter 5: Be Rich in Faith

W hen you think about money, there are so many things that come to mind that can silence your faith. If you are like me, you may wonder how something so small can cause such a big stink in the world! Yes, something that is no bigger than an index card has so much power over things that happen and, more importantly, people.

When we talk about our faith being vulnerable enough to be silenced, we have to consider the power of money. Unfortunately, Satan wants nothing more

"NEVER GIVE SOMEONE THE KEY TO UNLOCK YOUR SECURITY."

than to see us at our worst. The use of money is one of the easiest ways for him to do that if our faith is not where it is supposed to be.

One of the most telling stories in the Bible about money and faith is the Parable of the Talents found in the Gospels of Matthew and Luke.

To summarize, there was a master that was set to travel. So, he called over his three (3) servants that worked for him and gave each of them a talent according to their abilities. Now, in this day, a talent was equivalent to up to 16 years-worth of pay. Can you imagine being paid a salary like that up front? Imagine how many lives would be changed with something that significant!

The first two servants took their share and put it to work. The last servant decided to dig a hole in the ground and bury or hide what he had received.

When the master came back, he asked what became of the talents that he gave them. One of the servants said that he gained five talents more than what he was given. The second said he received two talents more. The servant that hid his talents told the master that he did it out of fear.

The master was happy with the two servants that put their monies to work and he actually promoted them. However, he was not as happy with the last servant and he actually banished him from his house.

Essentially, Jesus is explaining in this parable that those who have will be given more, while those who have nothing, everything will be taken away from them. Because of the fear that the servant expressed through his hiding, instead of being faithful with what he was blessed with, he ended up with nothing.

The fear of not having money can make you a slave to your own mind.

There have been times in my life when money was scarce. I can think of one time in particular when I got brave and started my own business full-time, as I mentioned in a previous chapter.

I created a small consulting company that focused on management and communications. With this company, I did everything. I was the president and CEO, the business developer, the marketing and communications person, and the administrative person. Everything depended upon me!

Starting out, I did a great job in getting my name out there to potential business partners. Having a background in marketing and communications, coming up with flyers, presentations, and promotions was second nature. I even sought out certain certifications to help boost the reputation of the business. Every morning was refreshing knowing that I was in charge of me! So, I thought.

There was mild success. I had a few opportunities that came through; one, in particular, that was pretty lucrative thanks to some great people. However, the key to being in business is understanding that you have to stay two steps ahead. When one project or contract is starting, another one should be close to being finalized. This was the part that I did not pray about or understand, at the time.

As a result, the money dried up and it was not coming as fast. I depleted savings accounts. I exhausted my 401K and a life annuity where I had accrued cash value. It was really a stressful time.

After months and months, I just remember breaking down in the middle of the floor and crying out to God, "WHY??!!" Tears were plentiful and flowing like rivers that never ended. It was the lowest point of my life. I had nothing in my accounts and did not know where my next dime was coming from. It was at this point that the thought of not existing anymore came to my mind. Feeling like a failure. Feeling like I did not accomplish anything and not seeing a way out. I let the devil put fear in my mind.

But God! Psalm 34:4 says, *"I sought the Lord, and he answered me; he delivered me from all my fears."* My praying to God and seeking His guidance led me to something that changed my life.

One morning, I woke up extra early. While lying in bed, I decided to look at the latest news on my iPad. While plowing through the business section, I stumbled upon an article about a local woman, minority-owned small business that had recently received a small business award. I was intrigued because it was a marketing and communications company – exactly what I did. Except, this company was doing much better than I was doing.

God gave me the idea to write an email to the CEO and ask for a business lunch to introduce myself and talk about possible opportunities to work together. At this point, there was no fear. There was nothing to lose. So, I wrote the email and the CEO answered me. With no hesitation, the lunch meeting was scheduled at a local restaurant in Washington, DC.

The meeting went really well. Although I went into the meeting to talk about partnerships with our businesses, God steered the conversation to a possible job opportunity. Sure enough, I ended up working for the CEO as a government consultant. Because I did not let the devil silence my faith, this lunch…this unexpected business opportunity turned into a blessing that forever changed my life and I will always be grateful.

Turn your doubting into touting and watch the blessings unfold.

Financial blessings are wonderful blessings to receive. It means that God has given you the ability to sustain yourself. You have the means to buy food for your family, pay your rent or mortgage, purchase clothing for you and your family, or make upgrades to your home. Whatever needs may exist, God allows your needs to be met. He does not want to see you be without. However, desires are totally different. Whatever the desires of your heart, if God sees fit that you have remained faithful and that you can handle the blessings, He allows your desires to be fulfilled.

Relating to the parable of the talents, the servant that held his money did not handle his blessing correctly. He allowed his faith to be silenced and let fear overtake him. It could have been the fear that he was not as good as the other servants to make his money work for him to increase it. Maybe it was a fear that because he did not believe in himself and his abilities, he might not see that level of money ever again. Perhaps, he just simply wanted to hoard his money. Although we do not know the true reason for why he hid his money, we know that many of us can go through a point of fear such as these examples that can hold back our future blessings.

There are times when we are in need and the financial blessings may not be there. When this occurs, our human nature begins to point us in the direction of worrying, stressing out, and eventually becoming doubtful. This is what the devil wants from us. If our faith is not where it should be, if our spiritual maturity is not where it should be, we can actually create a spirit of fear and doubt what God can do. For the devil, this is like a shark smelling blood in the water.

When Jesus resurrected and appeared before the Disciples for the first time, He could see that Thomas was

still in doubt that it was really Him. Think about all of the
miracles that Thomas witnessed while following Jesus. It
did not matter. He still had an overabundance of doubt,
even looking Jesus in the eye after the resurrection. This
doubt kept him from believing in the miracle of salvation.
How many of us have let doubt creep into our minds about
the validity of salvation?

Jesus had Thomas put his finger in His side where He
was pierced on the cross. John 20:27 says, *"Stop doubting
and believe."* This was Jesus's words to Thomas. Jesus is
showing us that this is what we have to do to not let the
devil silence our faith and give voice to doubt. Just stop
doubting and believe. You can tell when your faith has
increased because you feel that you have relinquished
control to God. You can literally feel it! Think about our
cruise control feature in our cars. We click that button and
it automatically takes control of the car. That is how our
faith should operate all the time.

When we let our doubt take over during times of
financial stress, sometimes unknowingly we can create
other gods that we serve. It can be purchasing lottery
tickets, going to casinos to gamble, getting involved in
quick money schemes that we did not pray on before
entering, or doing something illegal in some cases. We can

fall victim to many things leading us down a road that is not ordered by God.

In the midst of our storm while waiting for financial blessings, we have to turn our doubting into touting. Meaning, we must continue to give God the praise and have faith that God is working on our behalf. Remember, God's ways are not our ways and things will happen in His time; not ours.

We must not silence our faith while waiting for God to bless us with financial means. What we need to do is to stick our fingers in His side! Continue to tout what God has done for you and what God can do. Even continue to bless your place of worship and others financially with a sincere heart. If you remain faithful and do not silence your faith, I guarantee you that blessings will unfold!

Never give someone the key to unlock your security.

When it comes to being blessed financially, we can be our biggest obstacle. Our own insecurities can create an oasis of obstacles that, if we let it, can become a reality.

According to the American Psychological Association, insecurity can be multi-layered. The many faces of insecurity can include not believing in your abilities or your skills. Additionally, it can include not believing in your value as a person or your self-worth. For this section, let's focus on the last two layers.

Regarding financial blessings and our security, the devil wants nothing more than to let our past weigh us down to affect how we feel about ourselves. He is hoping that we will feel so bad about our self-worth that we will silence our faith and give up on God.

In our professional life, there are times where we go through certain scenarios that can cause us to question our value and self-worth. For example, we can put all of our efforts into a certain project and lead it with all the professionalism in the world. We can do everything correctly, make sure everything is under budget, and really have a cohesive team around us to execute everything.

Depending on the environment, we can encounter people who may question what we are doing and how we are doing it. Additionally, we can have difficult people on the project that just want to be an obstacle to us because we are running the show or they just do not like us. Furthermore, sometimes we run projects and we may not receive any recognition or mention or even a simple thank you for our efforts. Don't fall for the trap!

All of these things are small little keys that the devil can use to make us feel bad about our self-worth and value as a person. How we handle these situations may affect our ability to be blessed financially. If we act out in retaliation to any of these negative situations, we can potentially affect our ability to receive a bonus or some sort of financial incentive, or, in some cases, we can even be overlooked for a promotion.

When we fall for the trap, we throw ourselves into a psychological situation where we doubt our value as a person. If these accumulate over time, it can really pile up on us and our mental well-being.

However, God wants us to remember that we are His handiwork. Ephesians 2:10 says, *"For we are his workmanship, created in Christ Jesus for good works, which God prepared beforehand, that we should walk in them."* Never believe that you are not good enough! Be rich in faith and not fear. Know that we are conquerors in Christ.

Chapter 6: Lean On Faithful Promises

Is faith simply a bridge to a promise? Some people may see it that way. However, the problem with this thinking is that when the promise is not fulfilled, what does the person then feel about faith and its purpose? Does their faith become silenced?

There are so many promises made by man that have been broken. If you are not mature in your faith, your spirituality, or your relationship with God, you can fall victim to believing that broken promises can lead to a belief that faith is not real. Therefore, eventually your faith can become silenced.

"THE PROMISES OF GOD NEVER FAIL."

Health disparities in this country are at an all-time high. Citizens are having to decide between health, food, rent, or simply just existing. The COVID-19 pandemic heightened the issue of health disparities between those with money and those that may be less fortunate, disenfranchised, or economically disadvantaged. Many people believe that the promises of this country for equal justice for all have fallen short. Can the broken promises be put back together? The answer to that is neither here nor there.

The promise of economic justice has not been fulfilled for many. Some people have had faith in political people and agendas that promised they would move up in economic status, to no longer live in poverty, move to the middle class, or become a part of that 'one percent'. These promises have fallen short. Can the broken promises be put back together? The answer remains a mystery.

The racial divide in this country is like a cancer cell that surfaces, then becomes somewhat dormant or not as visible but then resurfaces and comes back stronger than ever. I am not comparing the experience of having cancer to race relations, but using a simple analogy about the visibility of race in our country.

The promise of seeing people for who they are and not what they are continues to be broken. Although some progress has been made in some areas, many areas still remain challenged or have worsened. Can the broken promises be put back together? The prognosis is still out with the jury.

God's word is filled with promises. Words of promises to deliver us. For example, Isaiah 43:2 says, *"When you pass through the waters, I will be with you; and when you pass through the rivers, they will not sweep over you. When you walk through the fire, you will not be burned; the flames will not set you ablaze."*

The difference in God's promises versus man-made promises is that God's promises are already ordained. Man-made promises are dependent upon what man wants to do that may or may not happen. It depends upon how man feels and how influenced he is by outside noise. God's promises are going to happen no matter what. All God wants us to do is to simply be faithful that just maybe one of those promises could be for us.

So, let's take a deeper look into promises based on the text of reference for this chapter.

Many people do not know that I once was a Cub Scout. Although I was not in it for very long, I did get to learn certain things. Some as simple as tying different kinds of knots. This helped me greatly once my dad started teaching me to tie my own necktie.

As a Cub Scout, you had a motto just like the Boy Scouts have a motto. Our motto started off with the words "I promise…" and continued with "to do my best, to do my duty to God and my country; to help other people, and to obey the law of the pack." This motto was recently changed to something different in 2015. Just like everything else, they have removed or are trying to remove God from basic things in life.

The word 'promise' is defined in the dictionary as a declaration. It is something that someone declares to do a task or a deed for somebody. The purpose of a promise is to also provide an assurance that something will happen. With a promise, people usually expect whatever is communicated to happen without a doubt. Promises also come in words of affirmation. For example, "I promise to love you always."

There are numerous examples where God displays His love for us through promises. In particular, the scripture reference for this chapter identifies a number of examples of His love through promises and takes us through various levels of promise.

The first level says that He will be with us when we 'pass through waters.' You may be saying "what exactly is going through waters about?" If I could identify an example of what going through waters could look like, I would look back at a time in my life where I experienced some difficulty.

I had moved out on my own for the first time to a nice bachelor pad apartment. It felt good to be on my own. I felt I was a real man by taking care of myself and handling things without mom and dad being around. Now, keep in mind that I did stay on campus while in college; however, having your own place was totally different and pretty liberating.

Well, as with anything in life you can easily become complacent as time moves on and living on your own is not exempt. One month, I made the mistake of spending a little more than I had; not to mention, my car surprisingly decided to act up and repairs were eminent.

I think about this particular time as 'going through waters' because I became behind on my rent over the span of two months. It was to the point that one day I arrived home from work and saw a notice on my door. Turns out it was an eviction notice left by the local sheriff. Now I know how the Evans family felt on Good Times all those times!

I had no clue what I was going to do. Could I go to my parents and explain that I was trying to live a lifestyle of the rich and famous? Since I was on my own, I had to be the man that I was claiming to be.

As a result, I ended up going to the bank to see if I could get a line of credit. Well, that did not work out too well. My last desperation was something that no one should ever do – get a payday loan!

The good part is that I was able to pay my back rent off and get back on track; however, I still had to go through the waters of paying back my payday loan and dealing with a shortage of money until I could get back on my feet.

The second part of the scripture speaks about how God promises to be with us so that rivers will not sweep over us.

As you can see, we go from 'waters' to 'rivers' which means that things in life are not always going to be just a little difficult. Things can and will get worse if you just keep on living.

There was a relationship that brewed with a young lady where we became pretty serious. She was very deep in God. So much so that she wanted to write gospel songs. Her father and mother were ministers. She grew up in a particular faith denomination different than I. Being young in our ages, we already had some differences of opinions about religion.

Some of those differences included tithing. Her faith in tithing was already at a place of maturity, whereas my faith in tithing, at this time, had not reached her level yet. Additionally, we visited a few churches as she did not have a church home where we lived. One church we visited, there was conversation with some of the members after the service. The topic of speaking in tongues came up. When I said that this was something that I had not experienced yet, the person looked at me like I had three heads. It was one of the most uncomfortable feelings I have ever had.

In the body of Christ, this is one of the things that we have to be careful about because we can contribute to silencing someone's faith by not making them feel welcome. When we perpetuate a feeling of superiority or inferiority on the people we come across, that may be young in faith, we can do more damage than we know.

This relationship was my 'river'. Outside of religious discussions, everything in the relationship seemed to be fine. However, after meeting her parents (the ministers), I think there was some discussion about me and my character or how well I would fit in the family. Nevertheless, our relationship did not last. It was the first time I really had someone I was in a relationship with really question my character because of differences in religious views or not having the right maturity level for religion.

Not to mention, my values about relationships focused on coming together and building together. With her, she wanted everything to be perfect at that point. This was something that went against my values for relationships. I believe that a man and a woman should come together and grow together, strengthening each other where they are not as polished and complimenting each other where different. She wanted a 'microwave' love. There was no room to grow or experience the building of something special.

This relationship could have swept over me like a river where I could have easily given up on love and silenced my faith in love. But, holding fast to my belief in loving someone through God's eyes and growing together led me to meeting and marrying my beautiful wife years later.

Lastly, the scripture elevates again in God's promise that He will be with us 'through the fire' and to not be afraid.

Probably my most life-changing event, other than my wedding, was the time that I had a serious health challenge. This was not too long after I started my company and then went back to work, as was mentioned earlier. I think the stress really took a toll on me. Stress is no joke!

During that unemployment period, in addition to the stress, I had become idle and was not moving a lot after the money slowed. I did not think my not having a job would affect me the way it did. The thinking was why did I need to get up early to be so mobile? It was not like I had anywhere to go. However, I do believe a mild form of depression did take a toll on me and did affect me.

Nevertheless, recognizing that I was not myself, I tried to get back out there and play some basketball. I could tell that I was out of shape. What made it worse was that I tried to dunk and failed miserably. I'm 6'2" and I used to be able to get up there! I knew I was not the same physically and something had changed.

After helping someone move one day, the next morning, I woke up and my legs were completely numb. I was scared to death. I did not know what to do. Eventually, I was able to crawl out of my bed and on to the floor. By moving around a bit more in a different direction, the feeling started slowly coming back to my legs. It was the weirdest feeling that I had ever felt in my life.

Still going through everyday life, I could tell my legs were not as strong as they once were. One day, I was getting out of my car and the slightest twist of my hip, I heard a pop in my hip. It got my attention, but, again, everything seemed okay so I did not think about it anymore.

As the weeks went on, my walk starting changing. It began to hurt to walk on one side. As it got colder, I noticed my leg did not want to move as much. It was some of the most excruciating arthritic-type pain I had ever felt.

After some doctor visits it was determined that I had blood vessels that were shattered in my hip and it was deteriorating. The pain when I walked was a combination of bone-on-bone and arthritis, as well as a damaged hip. The pain was so bad that sometimes it hurt to try and step up on the curb or step to get in the house.

The only thing that would make this pain go away was to have a hip replacement.

Here I am in my 30's considering a major surgery. Mind you, I had never been in the hospital. Mind you, Michael Jordan was still playing ball at this age! But now I have to contemplate getting a life-changing operation in order to have a better quality of life.

This was my 'fire.'

More tears came. More prayers went up. The more I talked to God, the more He assured me that this was the best step and that everything would be alright. My faith was expanded tremendously at this point. I was ready for the pain to be over and decided to move ahead with the surgery. I joke because there was also some assurance in that my doctor's last name was King! After all of the rehab was done, over time I learned to deal with it. To this day, I do not fully understand why *this* cross I had to carry, but having the replacement was the best decision and God delivered me from that pain. Of course, I cannot do all of the things that I once did athletically; however, the important thing was that my God kept His promise and did not let me die in this 'fire.' The same God that I serve can also do these things for you, too.

Believing in promises from God requires faith. When I wanted to write this chapter, one of the things that came to mind was a cartoon. I know…I can hear you saying 'cartoon??' Seriously, this cartoon really models what it means to have a level of faith that was exponential. The cartoon that I am speaking about is The Great Pumpkin Charlie Brown from The Peanuts franchise.

If you have seen this cartoon over the years, you know that Linus is sitting in this pumpkin patch and he has heard about this awesome being called The Great Pumpkin. It supposedly comes around every Halloween and those that are lucky to see him in the pumpkin patch will receive a lot of candy and other treats. It is truly a silly cartoon!

The interesting thing that applies to this chapter is not the fictional being or the celebration of Halloween. It is strictly Linus's faith in that this being will be coming before the night is over. Charlie Brown, Lucy, and eventually Sally - all of Linus's friends thinks he has gone bonkers and lost his mind!

I can still remember the end of the cartoon when Sally, who stuck by him the whole night, decides to leave because she missed a whole night of trick-or-treating waiting with Linus for the Great Pumpkin, because he never showed up. As she is leaving, she is yelling at him and calling him everything but a child of God!

What is amazing is that throughout the cartoon you can hear Linus yelling out "...just wait...you'll see; the Great Pumpkin will be here soon!" Even after Sally has yelled at him, Linus still expresses his conviction that the Great Pumpkin will come.

What if we had a Linus-type of faith with God? What if we leaned on God's promises with this type of faith? If we decided to go outside in the middle of the day and started screaming, "Jesus is coming back! Just wait...you'll see!", would our co-workers or neighbors think we have lost our minds?

This can sometimes seem difficult because of how we let down our guards and put our faith in man to deliver on the promises that are spoken.

Here is a key point that I do not want you to miss. You see, the problem with promises is not how a person expecting to receive the good deed or task perceives whether it will happen or not; the problem is with the person that is actually communicating the promise. What happens when the promises made by man are not kept?

Are we scorned? Do we become angered and full of wrath? What happens when we realize man has let us down? Well, we tend to no longer believe in that person. We may curse them out, try to get back at them, or we may just do nothing and write them off altogether.

Now, oddly enough, when promises are not kept, there's something harder that takes place. When promises are not kept, we may begin to give up on faith and silence it. Therefore, believing in faith when promises are not kept requires…you guessed it – more faith!

I am reminded of a story that I want to share with you. There was a young man named Jericho. He had a strange encounter one day that changed his whole perspective of life and let him know that God's promises were real.

One morning, he woke up at a normal time. His morning was going pretty ordinary just like other mornings. He decided to get ready to start his day.

Jericho got into the shower. About midway through his shower, he began to choke on his own saliva. He began to cough; however, there was nothing but steam. Jericho could not catch his breath so he came out of the shower gasping! It took him a while but he was finally able to catch it by breathing in some fresh air. It was one of the scariest moments of his life because he felt like it was the end.

Since then, Jericho was different. It was as if he looked death in the eye for the very first time and his perspective on things changed. He thought about the promises he made to people and the things he wanted to do in life. With a blink of an eye, all of that was almost a memory.

This experience taught Jericho that God promised him a new day. He was promised new life. Whatever he was thinking, whatever grudges or bad thoughts he was housing, it was time to get rid of them. God promised him another day and it is something he will never take for granted ever again. Do you take the promise of every day for granted?

Chapter 7: Master Your Faith

C an you really master the art of faith? I am willing to believe that this is a question a lot of people really do not think about. Although it may be seldom thought about, it is really an important question to consider when you think about everything we go through in our lives. Especially if we want to avoid our faith being silenced by the world, it behooves us to think seriously about how we can master it. No matter how you look at it, faith can be really hard to master. This is not a secret to anyone. But what does it take to master it?

Mastering your faith can take a few key things. It can take commitment, perseverance, and a whole lot of prayer.

"YOUR UNBELIEF CAN UNDO WHAT GOD WANTS DONE."

Even if we grew up in the church or have a decent foundation of Christian knowledge, we can find it difficult at times to master it. When life situations come and we think we have it covered, there is something that trips us up where it all can break down. The things that cause us to stumble can have us question if all the reading we've done, all the Bible studies we've participated in were really worth our time and effort.

If we stumble, sometimes we can recover pretty quickly and get back on track. But if we trip and fall, the devil has us right where he wants us and can attack us through our faith. This is why we have to learn to master it as much as we can. It takes practice and discipline.

The attacks we endure can allow discouragement and disappointment to feed into our faith and cause it to go silent. When this happens, there are two ways that we can deal with it. One, we can allow it to eat at our souls and totally destroy us; or, we can recognize that our God is greater than anything and continue to step out on faith knowing that He will never forsake us.

Fighting for our faith when under attack is something that takes heart. When we look at 2 Corinthians 4:16, it says *"Therefore, we do not lose heart. Though outwardly we are wasting away, yet inwardly we are being renewed each day."*

This scripture talks about not losing heart or not giving up. We can be under attack and our outward appearance can look like it has been through a heavyweight title fight. Remember the *Thrilla in Manila* between Joe Frazier and Muhammad Ali? This fight went 14 brutal rounds. How about the *Rumble in The Jungle* between George Foreman and Muhammad Ali? This fight only went eight rounds but they were extremely brutal rounds. In both of these fights, toward their end all of the fighters looked like you could push them over with a feather and they would fall to the canvas. Albeit a brutal experience, the fighters did not lose heart in the process.

Much like the fighters, when our faith is under attack, we have to roll up our sleeves and get down in the trenches, throwing whatever punches we need to at the enemy. There may be some blood and some bruising, but we continue to fight through faith. However, by fighting for our faith, inwardly we are being renewed and strengthened in the eyes of God. We can be so fixed on fighting the fight that we may not realize what God is doing for us on the inside.

This is how we start to incorporate commitment, perseverance and prayer into mastering our faith. Let's take a look at some other important ideas that will help us to master our faith so it will not become silenced.

What do you do to prep your faith?

Warmer weather means it is spring time! A time to spruce up the lawn, the flowerbed, or put some mulch around the trees. Perhaps, it is time to power wash the house, the fence, the deck, and the driveway. The garage has accumulated a lot of stuff. Maybe it is time to clean this out, too. Also, one of the most important things that may need attention is painting the house or touching up the paint in or outside the house.

If you are painting the house, there are so many things to prepare for before you actually do it. If the job is too large, then you may need to find a descent contractor to do the work. If it is being painted on the inside, then you have to make sure that furniture and other items are out of the way. Notably, you want to make sure you have the right paint with the right kind of gloss, and, of course, enough paint! However, probably the most important step to painting is ensuring that you use a primer.

What is that you may ask?

A primer is something that you put onto your painting surface, usually something in a neutral color, prior to painting. The purpose of the primer is to help seal any stains so that the new paint will stick better, in order to get the smoothest and cleanest finish possible. Much like painting, preparing our faith can work the same way.

Ephesians 2:10 says, *"For we are God's handiwork, created in Jesus to do good works, which God prepared in advance for us to do."*

As we go through life, so much can happen that can impact our emotional and mental well-being. Most likely, we will have some negative experiences that can leave us tainted, if we let them. Some of these experiences can even damage or stain our spirit where we give up on faith. There may come a point in time where God wants us to start priming ourselves to cover up the stains of life and get ready for the assignments that He has for us. So, what happens if we do not prep our faith?

Well, when we do not prime our painting surface, we run the risk of having the new paint we apply to the wall peel and not stick. This can happen especially when the conditions are warm or humid. Likewise, not prepping our faith can mean that we will not be ready for what God has for us. We will not be able to make it stick. Therefore, when things get hot for us in life (being tempted; being led in the wrong direction) our stains of life will continue to show. It will be difficult to overcome these things because our faith is not strong. So, how do we prep our faith?

We must realize that God has created us to do good works. The first way that we prep our faith is by immersing ourselves in the word of God with consistency. Some people think that when we say getting into the word of God it means 24 hours a day we are reading, praying, etc. Certainly, there is nothing wrong with doing that if you are able but we must be realistic about the time we have, the time we can take, and what may work best for us. For example, it is okay if you are just able to start out reading the Bible once a week and you gradually progress to a more consistent regiment. The key is to make a plan to do something and grow!

Another thing we can do to prep our faith is try and be around like-minded believers. There are a lot of people that may believe in Jesus Christ, but may not have a home church. They may not surround themselves in a community of believers. No one is perfect and there is certainly no perfect believer on this earth. We all sin and fall short of the glory of God. We must recognize that we are all growing in some way and it is good to have perspectives of different levels of faith to make us stronger.

The bottom line is that we have to accept that what happened in the past is just that – in the past. Whether we have been stained heavily or a little, whether we have suffered some emotional damage, God wants us to move forward. To do this, we must prep and prime our faith to get ready for the blood of Jesus that will paint our hearts to become the smooth and polished disciples that God wants us to become.

Your unbelief can undo what God wants done.

One of the things about ensuring our faith does not get silenced is that we have to realize when it is time to get out of our own way. When our spiritual confidence is low, one of the easiest things to do in our faith walk is to allow elements of doubt to enter into our minds and our spirit. Whether it is knowingly or unknowingly, we can become an obstruction of faith, if we are not careful. We can get in our own way instead of exercising our faith to help fulfill what God wants and has for us.

There is a passage in Mark that gives a striking example of how we can get in the way of our faith. Mark 9:23 says, *"If you can? Everything is possible for one who believes."*

This verse comes from a story where Jesus healed a boy that was possessed by an impure spirit. The father of the boy saw Jesus in the crowd and brought him over to Jesus. He began to tell Jesus all of the things that the boy experienced from the spirit. He then proceeds to ask Jesus, in a doubtful manner, "If you can do anything…"

The peculiarity here is that in the scripture, it says the man called Jesus "Teacher." Therefore, it is safe to say that the man already knew who He was and based on what he has heard about Him, he knew that Jesus was the only person that could help him. Jesus asks him "If you can?" He almost responds back to the man in disbelief, almost like Jesus is thinking (I'm paraphrasing here) *'are you serious? Don't you know who I am?'*

Think about the times in your life where you really needed something and you knew the very person who could help you. Did you let doubt creep into your mind? Did you ask with the hesitance of unbelief?

When we let our unbelief take over about what God can do, we can almost self-sabotage what we are trying to accomplish in the first place. A roadblock can be placed in front of the blessing we need. We stand in the way of our own faith and begin to undo what God wants for us.

If you have been on a sail boat before, chances are you have seen those gigantic ropes that are tightly tied around the bottom of the sails. These ropes help to keep the sails in place and if they become unraveled, the sails may throw the boat in a totally different direction. Like a ship with these ropes tied around the sail posts, we can allow our faith to become unraveled, causing the direction that God wanted us to go in, to be changed.

Emptiness has a cost.

One thing that can make mastering our faith difficult is our energy levels. We lead busy lives and sometimes we simply get tired. There is no doubt that a lot of us work very hard and still try to balance our daily life with our families. Additionally, whatever energy we have left, we try to extend to our churches, our communities, or other extra-curricular activities.

After the pandemic in 2020 and 2021, for some our energy levels have changed. They are not the same. As we try to get back into the swing of life prior to COVID-19, trying to do the same activities as before, there comes a point where we have to realize that the energy we try to expend is just not there. It is much easier to feel exhausted.

James 2:17 says, *"In the same way, faith by itself, if it is not accompanied by works, is dead."* Most likely, you are familiar with the phrase "faith without works is dead." This talks about how having faith alone does not do anything without some sort of action behind it. We can have all the faith in the world, but if we are not backing it up by helping someone, how does that help to move God's Kingdom forward? So, what fuels your faith?

When we put faith into action, our faith is often fueled by our personal desire to grow internally. There may be something that we want to change about ourselves and our character that we do not necessarily like. Or, someone has told us about ourselves to spark this change! By putting faith into action, we figure God will work on us on the inside.

Sometimes, putting our faith into action is fueled by our attempts to rewrite history – 'right' a 'wrong' that may have occurred with someone or some event in our lives.

For example, if a person did not have a fatherly presence in their household, they may want to do everything they can to give of their time to being a role model for youth. This person may see the value in becoming a foster parent, as a way to help someone not experience what they had to experience as a child.

Additionally, when we have doubts or low self-esteem about our relationship with God, we may try to put our faith into action in as many areas as possible. For example, we join different church committees, we may be in charge of a couple of ministries. This may also extend to supporting people we know in charge of certain ministries or nonprofit organizations. We take on the mindset to help, help, help!

Now, there is nothing wrong with having a serving heart. In fact, that is what God desires for us to do. However, when we expend ourselves across so many things, we can eventually burn out. It is now us who cry out help, help, help! This is why emptiness has a cost.

At the time this book was written, our country was dealing with high gas prices – some to the likes of which we have not seen in a long time. If you think about it, the more we drive our cars during this time and get closer to an empty tank, the more costly it will be for us to fill up.

The same thing applies to how we put our faith into action. The longer we go and the more we expend ourselves in so many different ways, we run the risk of burning out or, in some cases, even having health challenges. Additionally, we also run the risk of not being spiritually equipped. How, you say? Well, the more we are anywhere and everywhere, the more we dip into that time where we could be spending it with God. Reading. Praying. Fasting. When we are not in tune to God, we can ultimately risk not recognizing opportunities to bless someone with the *right* word from God. There is nothing more disheartening than having someone look to you as God's representative and you not be in a position to take them seriously or give them the right word they need to hear.

I am sure you have heard the phrase that you cannot pour from an empty cup. This is true. We must take care of ourselves, as well as our faith if we are to master it. If faith without works is dead, an empty faith can do more harm than we know.

Who are you letting in?

One of the most intriguing things about developing and mastering your faith is how you do this when it comes to your relationship with people. Friends, co-workers, potential business partners – you have to have a certain level of faith to really know who is in your corner. Life is hard as it is anyway. Without knowing who is on your side can present challenging situations in life, even some that can be adversarial. It is almost as if you are sitting prey.

1 Corinthians 15:33 says, *"Do not be misled: Bad company corrupts good character."*

One day I was watching a show about sharks. They are such fascinating creatures because you can never tell what they are thinking! One of the things I did not know is that sharks have a built-in sensor system called a lateral line. This line is a set of sensory nerves that run up and down the sides of the shark from head to tail.

Essentially, the lateral line is how sharks hear. You may say "how can sharks hear with sensory nerves down their body?" True, it does sound kind of weird. However, sharks do not hear like you or I. These sensory nerves allow sharks to hear through vibration. For example, if there is some drilling occurring in the ocean by some oil or aquatic or marine biology company, depending on the force of the vibration, it could cause sharks to stay away from that area.

In our spiritual walk to master our faith, we have to have the same type of sensory nerves that a shark would have to determine how to avoid people and things that might present bad vibes in our lives. To do this spiritually, we must learn how to do this through discernment.

The spiritual definition of discernment means we have the ability to perceive, without being judgmental, through spiritual guidance and understanding. We have insight into what God has for us and who God has for us in our corner. Discernment of God's will and discernment of spirits that we encounter every day. It would be unwise to simply believe that everyone we come across every day is someone good for our soul and spirit.

1 John 4:1 talks about how we should not fall into this trap of easy belief, naïveté or gullibility. It talks about how we need to test the spirits we encounter to see if they come from God. The way to do this is through prayer, making sure we study the Bible and exercising our gift(s) in areas of our lives. Most importantly, ensuring that we are obedient to God.

Just like the sharks that move away from the heavy vibrations felt in their lateral line, our discernment can protect us from bad vibes that can ultimately harm us.

Chapter 8: Content or Contentious?

The real meaning behind peace and being content is that, a lot of it really is not about what happens to us. It is how we recognize and handle the battle within ourselves to accept or not accept what happens to us. When we have difficulty recognizing and handling this battle, we can then come to develop a contentious spirit within ourselves.

Faith is about waiting and trusting while you wait. If you do not have patience, you cannot develop your faith. We must be more content rather than contentious

"CONTENTIOUS PEOPLE CHALLENGE YOU BECAUSE OF YOUR WEAKNESSES."

when it comes to faith. The more contentious we are or the more we come across contentious people, the more our faith can be silenced.

You can't walk with God, if you don't realize you're on a path.

One of the most important things that I speak about is how we have to pay attention to our journey. The path we take, the experiences – all of these things make up who we are in the sight of God. Therefore, if we are content with being numb to our journey, if we do not reflect on how God has blessed us or granted us mercy and grace, then it makes it very tough to walk with God. Not only does it make it tough to walk with God, when we do decide to walk, we may not know if we are walking in our right purpose because we are not locked in on God. This is something that could potentially silence our faith.

You are probably asking yourself "How can this make me contentious?" Well, it is quite simple. When we believe we are walking in a purpose that has not been validated by God, we may be approached by family, friends, co-workers, or even strangers in some cases. These individuals, through normal conversation, may be used by God to point out our true purpose. Because they may be connected (or not connected) with God, or someone who has totally realized their purpose, they can act as a conduit on behalf of God to help get us on track with our God-given purpose.

As a result, often times we can become contentious because we might feel that the person does not know what they are talking about. But, in all honesty, it may be the mere fact that we do not want to change from where we are most comfortable. We are content to be on the wrong path.

How many times have you felt good about what you thought was your purpose and someone else comes along with a different perspective of what your purpose should be? They pretty much pop our little bubble. We are contentious because it is something that we do not want to hear. The thing to be careful about is being content in the wrong purpose God has for us.

You can't be on the ropes if you don't get in the ring.

Have you ever had an individual just *'take you there?'* I do not mean going to a sporting event, a family gathering, a concert, or anything like that. I am talking about literally dealing with someone and letting them get under your skin. They *take you there.*

People that are contentious love to create an atmosphere of potential arguments or controversial actions. Most people operate contentiously because the more they can bring up the faults and issues of other people, the more it deflects the attention from their insecurities about their faults and issues. It is their way of creating a level playing field, albeit their level. We must be stronger and content with recognizing our own level of greatness as a child of God. When we fail to do that and follow contentious people, we downgrade our level of greatness, thereby reducing our faith in ourselves to be great.

Contentious people are going to challenge you. If they can sense a weakness in you or something about you that they can attack, they are going to do it. Especially in relationships, there can be much static between two people for whatever reason. And, if one of the individuals is more contentious than the other, they are going to try and dominate situations in the relationship. Some of these situations, we may not see them coming as there may not be any indicators or red flags. However, other situations, we allow ourselves for whatever reason to fall into these situations.

Proverbs 25:24 says, *"It is better to live on the corner of a roof than in the house with a quarrelsome woman."* Even though this scripture specifically mentions a 'quarrelsome woman,' a point can be made that this could speak to both men and women.

Contention in a domestic relationship can become toxic. According to the National Commission on COVID-19 and Criminal Justice, they released a report showing that "domestic violence incidents in the U.S. increased by 8.1% following the imposition of lockdown orders during the 2020 pandemic" *(Source: https://counciloncj.org/impact-report-covid-19-and-domestic-violence-trends/)*. The opportunity for contention in a household has increased.

I have been an advocate for a lot of things – education, civil and human rights, breast cancer awareness. However, one of the most intriguing things that I have advocated for is homelessness. Serving on a board for an organization that was the administrator for a homeless shelter was truly a rewarding experience. The shelter housed women and children who had experienced hardships. Hearing so many stories of their journey and struggles, I learned that many of them were leaving (or should I say escaping) situations of domestic violence. It was this very reason that we were not allowed to take pictures with residents in this shelter whenever there would be different events. It was truly a humbling experience but one that taught me a lot.

I am pretty sure that none of these women asked to be in that situation. There may have been some red flags that surfaced or there may not have been any at all. Nevertheless, a contentious atmosphere must have brewed in the households that led to the dissolution of the family.

One of the things we have to do is to work together better when it comes to domestic relationships.

Ephesians 4:26 says, *"Be ye angry, and sin not: let not the sun go down upon your wrath."* When we have difficulties in domestic relationships or marriages that surface, one thing we cannot do is to go to bed angry. This can lead to feelings and emotions simmering overnight that can end up exploding the next day or days later. Whatever is eating at you, try not to take it out on your significant other. Most importantly, do not sleep on it and let it fester. Apologize for any words that may have been insulting and out of character. Talk it out and get it to a point where you both can agree to speak upon it the next day.

Ephesians 4:32 says, "*And be ye kind one to another, tenderhearted, forgiving one another, even as God for Christ's sake hath forgiven you.*" One of the things that gets lost in domestic relationships is the fact that both parties are on the same team. This is the concept. It is not a competition and is not meant to be adversarial. It is a partnership that exists to glorify God – not ourselves. Where one is stronger, the other may be weaker. It is up to the couple to recognize their greatness together and work at it. That's right, I said WORK AT IT! It takes work. The more we keep God at the center of our relationships, the more we can realize that we all are on the same team and want the same happiness.

Allow yourself to make mistakes; but don't make the mistake of not learning from them.

We make mistakes. Big deal! Some of the greatest entrepreneurs, leaders, celebrities and entertainers have made many mistakes. Personally, I have made many mistakes in my life and I am sure you have a few, too.

Proverbs 1:7 says, *"The fear of the Lord is the beginning of knowledge; fools despise wisdom and instruction."* Mistakes are really just opportunities to grow. It is inevitable that we will make a mistake in life. There was only one perfect person that walked this earth and His name is Jesus. Yet, even He lost it in the temple courts when He drove out all who were buying and selling. It was like the money changers did not have any fear for the Lord.

When we make mistakes, sometimes we can forgo the lesson in the whole thing. Understanding what we did wrong, why it happened, or where the ball dropped that allowed the mistake to occur. Did the mistake really happen because of us? Or was it some outside force that caused it.

In the journey of life, our actions can sometimes create mistakes. Especially when we are not guided by God, our actions can lead us down the path to many blunders or slip-ups. Some of them may be small, they may be large, or they can be lifelong or even generationally impacting.

When we are wrong, we can be contentious in not adjusting anything to learn from our mistakes. This is because we do not fear the Lord. We can be very cavalier about some of our mishaps. They may have been mistakes where we keep going back to an ex from a rocky relationship. It may be choosing the wrong job to accept or not looking closely at the contract for something we are buying or obtaining a service. This may have happened more than once but we do nothing about fixing what we are doing. This can lead us down a dark road.

When we fear the Lord, we open up the possibility to gain knowledge that can help change our thoughts on these situations to help us avoid repetitive mistakes. However, if we do not recognize or ask God for help in our corrective actions, we become foolish about accepting instruction that can turn into wisdom. We can end up becoming contentious against ourselves! Many people do not want to be told what to do or how to do it. That is simply human nature. But, the more we ignore something that can potentially turn out to be the best thing for us, the more we turn a deaf ear to God, we can ultimately silence our faith.

Experiencing a setback simply means you have more room to grow.

A lot of times, when we experience a setback, we can think it is the end of the world. If it is something we really had our hearts set on, for it not to come through can put us in a different space. However, all we really need to keep in mind is that when we get moved back a few paces, this just allows us more room to step forward and grow.

1 Corinthians 15:58 says *"Therefore, my beloved brethren, be ye steadfast, unmovable, always abounding in the work of the Lord, for as much as ye know that your labor is not in vain in the Lord."*

When setbacks occur, we have to avoid contention and be content. There is a lesson in what has taken place and we need time for God to reveal it. We must continue to put our best foot forward and not let our faith be silenced. We cannot impulsively change the outcome to our favor. Instead, we need to turn our attention to the work of the Lord with the faith that He will reveal to us what our next move should be.

Chapter 9: Have a Mind-Blowing Faith

Have you ever been so amazed at something that God has done? Whether it was something for you or for someone else, did it really just blow your mind?

Our God has done some amazing things over time. We should always take the time to get to know God and His ways to understand the power that He possesses. So many miracles that have come directly from Him or from Him through Jesus Christ. Our God has done some awesome deeds that leave us in wonder!

If you are like me, you probably look back over your life and wonder how or why you are still here. Some of the things that have occurred, we may feel like we do not deserve to still be standing. However, we still stand because of the grace and mercy that God gives us each day.

"GOD WILL TURN THE SEAS OF YOUR LIFE INTO DRY LAND."

I have been held up at gun point, had a serious operation, been unemployed twice, and a number of other things that keep me in awe of the God we serve.

95

God has enemy-cringing power.

One thing that we must understand is that the power of God will stand up to any enemy. Just the mere mention of God will make enemies cringe and second guess whatever they are doing to promote evil.

In Matthew 4, Jesus was tempted by the devil in the desert. Satan taunted Him by daring Jesus to turn stone into bread. He tried to tempt Jesus to throw Himself down off a cliff to command His angels to save Him. Lastly, Satan tried to tempt Jesus with the riches of the world that Satan did not even own himself. But, the power of Jesus made the devil cringe to the point where he eventually fled. He is truly a liar and a manipulator, and will stop at nothing to deceive. If he has the audacity to try and tempt Jesus, what makes you think that the devil will not try to tempt you?

Colossians 2:15 says, *"He disarmed the rulers and authorities and put them to open shame, by triumphing over them in him."* The battles we face, we do not have to fight them alone. God wants us to have the faith to come to Him with our heavy burdens and turn them over to Him.

When we do not allow God to be the general of our battles, we try to fight for God and sometimes end up in a deeper mess than when the battle began. The more we discount the power of God in our battles and lose, the more it can begin to silence our faith.

God will turn the seas of your life into dry land.

We have to understand that when we exercise our faith and turn our battles over to God, the rough seas of our lives will no longer exist. The bumpy current becomes a dry space that is passable. We are able to survive!

Think about the Israelites delivered by Moses from Pharoah's bondage. In order to be delivered, God had to part the Red Sea so they could walk on dry land to their freedom.

In any situation in life, God is capable of doing anything to deliver us from the rocky seas of life. He will give us a path, but it is up to us to have faith and follow it.

Expect that God will blow our minds.

When we do everything on our own and leave God out of it, it is easy to lose sight of what faith is really about. The more we do it, the more our faith can become silenced by the world. We have to grow in our faith to a level of expectation from God that is humungous. We have to expect that God will do something in our lives to blow our minds. He will do something so miraculous that the average person will not believe it.

We have to have mind-blowing faith if we are to expect God to do mind-blowing things!

97

God does not want our faith level to appear like we are going through the motions. Do not have a lazy faith! We have to be sincere about our faith and exhibit transparency. Most of all, we must have a certain level of enthusiasm about believing in God's abilities that He will deliver us from anything. However, if we remain passive about our faith, we give Satan the opportunity to step in and affect our minds. Ephesians 4:27 says that we should not give the devil any kind of opportunity! He is just waiting to decrease our faith for his purposes.

Chapter 10: 'Uh·meh·ruh·kn' Idle

The year 2020 A.D. (or 2020) - It was supposed to be the year of vision for us all. A year of foresight. It was supposed to be the year where new things happened. 2020 should have been the year where the young woman or man decided to take a leap of faith and start their new business. It should have been the year where hundreds, maybe thousands, of couples decided to take their leap of faith and jump the broom. Maybe it was going to be the year that a recent college graduate felt a sense of hope and fearlessness about jumping into the "real world" and taking their career head-on.

It is true, the year 2020 was supposed to be a lot of these things to you and me, and maybe it was supposed to be so much more. But it was essentially a year where our faith could be silenced.

'Uh-meh-ruh-kuh' has had some tumultuous years on record, according to many historians. For example, 1861-1865 saw the Civil War create a lot of hard times. Also, 1929 saw the stock market crash, which led to the Great Depression in 1930. Some even consider 1968 a hard year, because of the deaths of Robert F. Kennedy and the Reverend Dr. Martin Luther King, Jr. which led to a lot of inner-city violence across the country. In 2001, the events of September 11th were the most difficult part of that year and led to so many changes to how we do things today.

Nevertheless, 2020 will probably go down as the most detrimental and undesirable year to remember in our generation. It is probably the most sickening and mentally draining year on record in the last century. I say this not only from the perspective of our country, but also from the perspective of the entire world.

You know how we like to buy champagne and wine as gifts to our family and friends for whatever occasion? I can almost guarantee you that there will not be many gifts of wine or champagne with the year 2020 on it! If you do receive one, you should probably re-evaluate your circle! This goes for cars, too. I do not think anyone will be buying a used car from 2020. After doing some research, the number 20 represents a cycle of wholeness where there is a period of labor, waiting or suffering that resembles a trial and reward.

From a biblical perspective, Jacob worked for Laban for 20 years after he was promised Rachel, but was tricked into marrying Laban's eldest daughter Leah. Solomon took 20 years to build a house for himself and God. Regarding, Abraham, God told him in their back-and-forth negotiation that if he found at least 20 righteous people in the cities of Sodom and Gomorrah, He would not ruin them.

So, there are some instances where 20 is prevalent in the Bible and suffering is involved. As a result, it is not uncommon to think that two "20's" would involve a lot of suffering and even loss.

The year was filled with many losses; some of a personal nature and some that had no direct connection to any of us. Fortunately, God blessed me in that I did not have anyone in my family succumb to COVID-19.

Although some of the losses may not have had a direct connection with us, some of them still hit us pretty hard.

For me, it started in January 2020 with the death of NBA basketball star, Kobe Bryant and his daughter Gianna. When I was growing up, Michael Jordan was my all-time favorite basketball player and to me, to this day, is considered as the G.O.A.T. (Greatest of All Time). I, too, was also pretty handy with a basketball! I played organized ball for the local boys and girl club, and eventually for the county where I lived although I never made my high school basketball team. I did play in the intramural league while at my alma mater – Bowie State University.

However, when Michael Jordan left the game, Kobe Bryant was in command of the league. In my humblest of opinions, I believe Kobe Bryant was the next best thing to Michael Jordan in terms of his athletic ability, his intensity, being a clutch player, and how he approached the game. In fact, it is believed that Kobe Bryant actually studied Michael Jordan because of his admiration for him. I guess he really wanted to "be like Mike," as did I at one time.

Of course, there were other notable losses, such as Chief Justice Ruth Bader Ginsburg, Chadwick Boseman (Black Panther), NFL Hall of Famers Don Shula and Gale Sayers, rock legend Eddie Van Halen, Alex Trebek, Congressman John Lewis, and many, many more.

Another loss was the symbolic and amplified loss of justice, and the belief that the lives of black and brown individuals did not matter.

One of the most outraged events of injustice in 2020 came when George Floyd, a black man whose death became a rallying cry across the country, was murdered in Minneapolis, MN by a police officer who used a knee restraint technique on Floyd's neck for 8 minutes and 46 seconds. It was later testified by others in the Minneapolis Police Department that this technique was not taught in the training academy.

I must admit; I was outraged and furious as I watched the video with the officer's knee on the windpipe of Mr. Floyd for such a long period of time. Not only was my feeling one of outrage, but it was also one of mixed emotions of sadness and hopelessness.

Many times, have we seen the stories of death by injustice through the eyes of Trayvon Martin, Michael Brown, Sandra Bland, Eric Garner, Philando Castile, Breonna Taylor, Ahmaud Arbery, and Tamir Rice to name a few. Even the horrible massacre at Emanuel African Methodist Episcopal Church in Charleston, SC, in 2015, where nine individuals lost their lives, we saw the injustice of the local police apprehending the killer and taking him to get something to eat on the way to the police station.

I do not have to tell you about the number of stories that we have seen that tell the story of death by injustice. Can you, however, imagine the ones that were *not* filmed? However, the death of George Floyd just hit differently. It put people of color on a roller coaster of emotions where it was difficult to process what happened, why it happened, and how we should feel about it and what action to take.

My heart truly goes out to his family for having to endure such an ordeal. I know that there is nothing that will bring back Mr. Floyd - a former athlete, truck driver, and bouncer. What many people did not realize, however, is that he was also known as a mentor in his religious community.

There is never anything good about any tragedy; however, if there was any good that could come out of such a tragedy as this, it is that not only did this put people of color on a rollercoaster of emotions, but it also stirred up a sense of preponderance of disbelief and confusion in people of non-color about why this happened and continues to happen.

Due to the faith of a number of people, George Floyd's death sparked a movement of conversations on race through protesting and speaking out on racial inequality in 'Uh-meh-ruh-kuh' and throughout the world. Their faith could not be silenced.

Finally, the handling of COVID-19 (Coronavirus) and the political scene in 2020 was a culmination of chaos that spewed over into life. There is no other way to say it. It was a perfect storm to all of the things that hold the country down – injustice, health disparities, and political dysfunction. If 'Uh-meh-ruh-kuh' were to just fix these three things, imagine what kind of country this would be!

Instead, we had leadership that infused fires of hatred and subliminal messages to its supporters in contradiction of these things, in order to carry out acts of hatred through physical threat and policy.

This perfect storm led to an 'Uh-meh-ruh-kuh' that was completely idle.

The irony in all of this is that while we were idle, our faith was being tested because we were losing idols, many were following an idol, and we were susceptible to becoming spiritually idle.

When I think about 2020 and the perfect storm that affected a number of us in different ways, I cannot help but to think about the book of Exodus and the Israelites being led by Moses out of bondage from under Pharaoh in Egypt. The reason why is because the Israelites' faith was tested after Moses delivered them.

To know how this book in the Bible relates to this chapter, you must understand a little about gods and idols. Some people may view an idol as a man-made symbol or image of something. It may not emulate the god itself, but may possess a characteristic in which someone elevates that image to a high level of importance.

Then, there are some people who may view an idol as something with great power and dominance of a god. The difference here is that this idol actually becomes the object of worship.

In Exodus, there is a stark contrast between the god (a golden calf) that the Israelites made while Moses was away on Mount Sinai waiting to receive the Ten Commandments from the God of Israel.

The Israelites began to doubt the faith that got them out of Egypt and on the road to the Promised Land. They never took hold of it, because they lost sight of the God of Israel and needed a man-made golden god or idol to accommodate their belief. Their ignorance and dismissive attitude toward their faith in God cost them the Promised Land and therefore the Israelites wandered in the wilderness for 40 years.

The oddity in contrast is what began this exodus. The fact that Moses was called to a burning bush where he received instruction from God to lead the mission to deliver the Israelites from Pharaoh's hold. The most important thing to understand, however, is that Moses could not look at God in His face. He was truly afraid.

Moses's faith led him to a conversation with God, without looking at Him, in which he had no clue of what God was going to ask of him. Without looking Him in the face, Moses was assured of his mission. He did not need to see God in order to get direction. His faith led him to believe that this indeed was God talking to him.

The Israelites, after being delivered out of bondage, no longer had faith in this same God that brought them out, but needed to *see* an image of something to continue to be assured of some level of freedom.

How many of us need to see signs from God in order to believe everything will work out? We need to be careful about this because this kind of thinking goes against the intended purpose of faith and often times why our faith becomes silenced.

We must be careful to not discount the power of faith, because when we look for signs to see evidence of God, we may end up following the wrong person, if we do not know the voice of God for ourselves. Whenever we follow the influence of someone that is not being guided by God, we begin to hold their image or the idolatry of them to a higher standard; a higher level of importance than necessary.

This can make you spiritually idle.

Similar to how the Israelites were punished by God to wander for 40 years in the wilderness, our idle faith can cause us to wander until God is convinced that we should be brought out.

The same could be said about our time being spent in the pandemic and how we increased our relationship with God during that time. What did we do to increase our faith? Did we increase our prayer life? Did we take on a new mission or work closely with a ministry or non-profit organization to help those in need? During our wandering through the pandemic, how have we increased our faith in order to be ready when God chooses to bring us out completely?

The idle 'Uh-meh-ruh-kuh' we live in today is a result of the chaos of 2020 and other things that have built up to that point. The reason why 'Uh-meh-ruh-kuh' is spelled this way is because the country we live in is almost unrecognizable.

Additionally, it is as a result of these things coupled with people following the wrong people – those that have not been led by God. It is a result of looking for something to believe in that has been perpetuated to a higher standard that is not ordained by God.

As we move to get 'Uh-meh-ruh-kuh' back on track, it is my sincere hope that we have all increased our faith level during this time to be the vessels that God needs us to be. We have to move this idle 'Uh-meh-ruh-ka' forward.

Inspiration for a Week of Faith

The following statements are to provide guidance throughout the week on how to approach your faith.

<u>SUNDAY</u>

A Chosen Purpose

John 15:16 *"You did not choose me, but I chose you and appointed you so that you might go and bear fruit – fruit that will last – and so that whatever you ask in my name the Father will give you."*

We all have a purpose that has been ordained by God. One that is not self-serving, but helps God's Kingdom to grow and prosper. If we are not doing what we have been called to do, our blessings can be delayed. Don't get me wrong, our needs will always be met by God, if we believe and have faith. But the desires of our heart, that we ask for in the name of Jesus, may be on hold until we begin to fulfill our purpose.

MONDAY

Don't Sit on Your Testimony

John 5:11 "But he replied, "The man who made me well said to me, 'Pick up your mat and walk.'"

When Jesus healed the man to walk again, taking the mat with him was meant to be a constant reminder of where he had been in his life. Not to be burdensome in thought, but with the hope that anyone whom he encountered might know the power of our Lord. Are you still sitting on your mat after God has brought you out of something? Do not sit on your testimony. Get up and walk! Be a faithful blessing to someone else and let them know what God has done.

TUESDAY

Let It Go

John 14:1 "Do not let your heart be troubled. You believe in God; believe also in me."

The way to eternal life is only as secure as your trust in Jesus. Sometimes when a storm arises, we forget that our unwillingness to fully trust in Him is what may actually keep us in our storm. Whatever is eating at your spirit, be faithful and give it over to God. Let go and let God!

<u>WEDNESDAY</u>
It Ain't About You

James 4:6 *"But He gives us more grace. That is why Scripture says 'God opposes the proud but shows favor to the humble.'"*

It ain't about you! Boasting is not pleasing to God. What is pleasing is humbling yourself in attitude and service. If you act like you have it all under control all the time, you miss out on the opportunity to grow and move from prevenient, to justifying, to sustaining grace from God. Focus on being humble and watch your grace increase.

<u>THURSDAY</u>
Real Friends

Proverbs 27:6 *"Wounds from a friend can be trusted, but an enemy multiplies kisses."*

Have you ever had a friend to just break down some of your issues to your face? Those that truly care about you or consider you as a friend will be honest with you. They help you to be accountable when you are in the wrong. Those that want to see you fail will tell you exactly what you want to hear, if it means your demise. Pray for discernment of who is in your circle that values your friendship.

FRIDAY
C.H.A.N.G.E.

Revelation 21:5 *"He who was seated on the throne said, "I am making everything new!" Then he said, "Write this down, for these words are trustworthy and true."*

Christ Has A New Goal for Everyone. In other words, CHANGE is not about where you are in life. It is about what you are becoming. Do not focus or worry about what was and what may not be the same. Look forward and be faithful as to how you will be made new in the process.

SATURDAY
Who We Are

Ephesians 4:23 *"...let the Spirit renew your thoughts and attitudes."*

Where we come from helps to shape the character and strength of who we are; it does not define or serve as the catalyst of who we are to become.

SILENT FAITH
Finding Assurance In The Hidden

CPSIA information can be obtained
at www.ICGtesting.com
Printed in the USA
LVHW080056151022
730730LV00013B/250